DA IN THE WILDERNESS

THE ESSENTIAL GUIDE
TO HARD TIMES

by
Wm. W. Wells

2. David in the Wilderness

Published by William W. Wells

Copyright ©2020 by William W. Wells

Unless otherwise noted, all Bible quotes are from the NASB

ISBN: 979-864032-653-6

Table of Contents

4. David in the Wilderness

6. David in the Wilderness

CHAPTER 1: INTRODUCTION

And Samuel said to Jesse, "Are these all the children?" And he said, "There remains yet the youngest, and behold, he is tending the sheep." Then Samuel said to Jesse, "Send and bring him; for we will not sit down until he comes here" (1 Samuel 16:11).

How This Book Came About

Several years ago, I taught a series on the life of David for the youth at my church. The concept was to match the history of David, as found in First and Second Samuel, with relevant Psalms of David. In particular, I was interested in the Psalms which the Septuagint attached to specific historical moments in the life of David.

The series was meant to encourage open discussions with the youth in my class. The concept was to look at some of the salient points in the life of David, and to try to pry open what was going on in David's thoughts and feelings through a look at relevant Psalms. For this reason, I have included discussion questions at the end of each chapter. If you are using this book for personal study, use those questions to think more deeply about the thoughts and feelings that these events stirred up. Pay special attention to how David is developing the leadership skills that will one day make him a great king.

8.   David in the Wilderness

Originally the intention was to study the entire life of David, but circumstances shortened the project to David's life up to his triumphant return to Judah. Since there are very few psalms attached to specific events in David's life after his wilderness experience this mad sense anyway. The wilderness formed David, the king. The result was a deep dive into some of the more trying times in the life of Israel's future king.

Sitting in self imposed isolation, during the Covid-19 crisis, it occurred to me that this study might make a useful book concerning how we are meant to handle ourselves in difficult times.

The story of David begins with David being anointed king of Israel. Unfortunately, there is already a king of Israel who has an heir apparent ready to replace him when he dies. David from this point forward is living with a promise over his life, that doesn't appear to have any practical way of being fulfilled, outside of outright rebellion. He is no position to start a rebellion as we will see.

Anointing a Future King

Our first introduction to the future king is when the prophet Samuel is instructed by God, "Fill your horn with oil, and go. I will send you to Jesse the Bethlehemite, for I have provided for myself a king among his sons" (1 Samuel 16:1). Samuel is reluctant owing to the fact that Saul, the current king, whom he had anointed previously, is not likely to look kindly on Samuel anointing a new king (1 Samuel 16:1-2). God tells him to disguise the act as a simple sacrifice to the Lord.

> So Samuel did what the LORD said,
> and came to Bethlehem. And the elders
> of the city came trembling to meet him
> and said, "Do you come in peace?" He
> said, "In peace; I have come to sacrifice
> to the LORD. Consecrate yourselves
> and come with me to the sacrifice." He
> also consecrated Jesse and his sons and
> invited them to the sacrifice (1 Samuel
> 16:2-5).

There is tension between Samuel and king Saul. Samuel's last meeting with Saul ended with him telling Saul that "The LORD has torn the kingdom of Israel from you today and has given it to your neighbor, who is better than you" (1 Samuel 15:28). The elders of Bethlehem are nervous at the appearance of Samuel. The prophet tries to reassure them that he is not there to cause trouble, he is just there to sacrifice. His purpose is to anoint a future king, but this is a secret mission. It could be seen as a declaration of rebellion, so the matter is meant to stay private until God's timing is full.

When the great prophet arrives at the feast, Eliab, Jesse's eldest son, is presented before him. Samuel thinks, "Surely the LORD's anointed is before him." (1 Samuel 16:6). The current king Saul, whom Samuel had anointed originally, was very tall (1 Samuel 10:23). Here again was a tall and handsome warrior, surely, this young man would make an excellent king. But, God said, "Do not look on his appearance or on the height of his stature, because I have rejected him. For the LORD sees not as man sees: man looks on the outward appearance, but the LORD looks on the heart" (1 Samuel 16:7).

10. David in the Wilderness

One by one, Jesse parades each of his seven favorite sons before Samuel. One by one, God says no (1 Samuel 16:8-10). Seven sons are presented, but not one is chosen by God. Samuel is sure that he is hearing from God, so what is wrong?

Young David

Jesse, David's father has not intended to present David, nor has he even called David to be present to see one of his brothers honored. It is likely that David knows little of what is happening. Samuel is not interested in Jesse's thoughts on the matter, he is only interested in God's thoughts on the matter.

> And Samuel said to Jesse, "Are these all the children?" And he said, "There remains yet the youngest, and behold, he is tending the sheep." Then Samuel said to Jesse, "Send and bring him; for we will not sit down until he comes here" (1Samuel 16:11).

We know David as the great king of Israel. But as a young boy, David was not getting the vote as most likely to succeed. We don't know many details, but we do know that he was constantly tending the sheep, while there is never a mention of his brothers doing the same. When the brothers go to war, David is sent to bring them supplies. It would appear that he was treated more like a servant than a son. Was there some reason why he singled out? We don't know. What we do know is that when Samuel arrives to anoint a new king, Jesse calls his seven older sons, but not David.

When David appears, the first thing that Samuel notices is that he was ruddy (1 Samuel 16:12). David spent most of his time out of doors. Samuel looks on this bright-eyed young man, and God says "Arise, anoint him, for this is he" (1 Samuel 16:12).

Samuel anoints David, and the Spirit of the LORD rushes upon the boy (1 Samuel 16:13). Now you would think that David's stock would have risen sharply in the family circle, but keep reading. Saul needs a psalmist, one who is skillful at soothing him when he is agitated. David's name is mentioned and so David is sent for. Where is he? David is still with the sheep (1 Samuel 16:19).

Maybe David was just there training a replacement. Well, turn to the next chapter. The Philistines gathered for war. Goliath, a giant man of war stands as the champion of the Philistine army. The Israelite army is terrified of him. David's three oldest brother's Eliab, Abinadab, and Shammah are sent to join Saul's army (1 Samuel 17:13). David serves Saul as a psalmist, but also continues to go back and forth to Bethlehem to feed his father's sheep (1 Samuel 17:15). It was common for those who served the king to serve for several months and then return home for the remainder of the year. After all that has happened to honor David, when he returns home, his family is still treating him like a servant.

And then comes the day that Jesse sends David on an errand: "Take now for your brothers an ephah of this roasted grain and these ten loaves and run to the camp to your brothers. Bring also these ten cuts of cheese to the commander of their thousand, and look into the welfare of your brothers, and bring back news of them. For Saul and they and all the men

of Israel are in the valley of Elah, fighting with the Philistines"
(1 Samuel 17:17-19).

Notice that there are still other brothers available to send, but
David is the one who is sent to carry supplies to his elder
brothers. His father Jesse has to explain to David what is going on. It appears that David is left so far out of the loop concerning family matters that Jesse has to tell David that three
of his older brothers have left to join Saul's army.

There seems to be a huge disconnect between God's valua-
tion of David and how he valued by his family and likely his
friends and neighbors. We assume that David's skill as a
shepherd was well known. The other thing that we do know
is that young David had an impressive reputation as someone
who could sing and play the harp. He was not only a great
musician, but he wrote his own psalms. It was likely that he
had become a great psalmist on all those lonely nights tending
sheep. In any case, he was now one of those who served king
Saul personally, singing and playing his harp. This should
have raised his reputation in the neighborhood.

Discussion Points:

1. What was David's value in the eyes of his family?

2. How do you suppose this affected his value in the eyes of his friends and neighbors?

3. Why do you suppose that God chooses David, above his brothers?

4. It says that the Spirit of the Lord rushed upon David (1 Samuel 16:13). What do you suppose that looked like? Do you think that his father and his brothers noticed?

14. David in the Wilderness

Application:

1. It appears that David's family did not value him very highly, even when he was being honored and respected by others. How do you think your family sees you? It seems that David suffered from low self-esteem due to his treatment. How do you see yourself?

2. We really don't know how David's friend's and neighbors thought of him. We do know that his skill with psalms was recognized, bringing him into Saul's court. How do you suppose the attitude of your closest friends and family affects your value in the eyes of other friends and neighbors? Does your own self-esteem affect how others see you?

3. David is chosen for a special place in God's kingdom. What do you think God sees in you? Do you think God has a special place for you in His kingdom? When you look at the people around you, do you think God has a special purpose for them? Have you told them so?

4. It says that when Samuel anointed David, the Spirit of God rushed upon him. Have you experienced the Spirit of God touching you in a personal way? What

do you experience in these moments? Are there specific ways that your body reacts? How do your thoughts and emotions react?

16. David in the Wilderness

CHAPTER 2: DAVID THE GIANT SLAYER

> Then David spoke to the men who were standing by him, saying, "What will be done for the man who kills this Philistine and takes away the reproach from Israel? For who is this uncircumcised Philistine, that he should taunt the armies of the living God?" (1 Samuel 17:26).

The Anointing

When David arrives at the front lines searching for his brothers, Goliath appears, sneering at the troops of Israel, and those troops fled from him cowering at his stature. "Have you seen this man", David is listening to the men exclaim, "the king will enrich the man who kills him with great riches and will give him his daughter and make his father's house free in Israel." (1 Samuel 17:25).

David is not intimidated by Goliath. His interest is peeked, "What shall be done for the man who kills this Philistine and takes away the reproach from Israel? For who is this uncircumcised Philistine, that he should defy the armies of the living God?" (1 Samuel 17:26). David begins in the way of the world, the way of the conversation in front of him, "What shall be done for the man…?" There are riches and honor to be gained.

18.   David in the Wilderness

David's vision starts self-focused, but his thoughts immediately shift. David envisions the man who "takes away the reproach from Israel", and finally indignantly asks, "who is this uncircumcised Philistine, that he should taunt the armies of the living God?" (1 Samuel 17:26). The anointing on David is enlarging David's heart. He no longer sees himself as a shepherd of sheep, even though his family still sees him in that role, he is now, without any worldly title or direction, the shepherd of Israel. It is contained in the destiny spoken over him when Samuel poured the oil of anointing over him. Looking down on this defiant Philistine before whom all of Israel cowered, it would seem that David heart "grew two sizes that day".

David's brother hasn't any idea of what is happening.

> Now Eliab his oldest brother heard when he spoke to the men; and Eliab's anger burned against David and he said, "Why have you come down? And with whom have you left those few sheep in the wilderness? I know your insolence and the wickedness of your heart; for you have come down in order to see the battle" (1 Samuel 17:28).

Eliab was present when Samuel anointed David, but it has had no impact on him. He is accusing David of playing hooky from his job, tending sheep. It is clear that Eliab has a low opinion of David.

Eliab, like the rest of the troops of Israel, sees the giant Philistine as a river too big to cross. David sees a giant who is insulting God's people, in front of God. David is embracing God's people, because God asked him to. I sincerely doubt that any of this is coming out of David because of some conscious deliberation on his part. His destiny has changed, so his heart's cry has changed. It just bubbles up like a fresh spring. This spring one has the fragrance of heaven in it.

Eliab's sneer takes David off guard, "What have I done now? Was it not just a question?" (1 Samuel 17:29). The situation before David, the situation before Israel, the situation before God, has pushed all of the normal family dynamics so far away that David seems to struggle to understand Eliab's taunt.

By some miracle of heaven, this young man is sent on behalf of the armies of Israel, not dressed for war, but dressed as a shepherd, staff in hand, with a pouch of stones and a sling (1 Samuel 17:40). The Israelites are undoubtedly wondering what is wrong with Saul's thinking, allowing David to step out on behalf of all Israel dressed as a shepherd. Saul is probably thinking the same thing. Goliath is fuming at the insult. But David is confident that he is there with God beside him.

> You come to me with a sword and with a spear and with a javelin, but I come to you in the name of the LORD of hosts, the God of the armies of Israel, whom you have taunted. This day the LORD will deliver you into my hands, and I will strike you down and remove your head from you. And I will give the dead bodies of the army of the Philistines this day to the birds of the sky and to the wild beasts of the earth, that all the

> earth may know that there is a God in
> Israel, and that all this assembly may
> know that the LORD does not deliver
> by sword or by spear; for the battle is
> the LORD'S and He will give you into
> our hands (1 Samuel 17:45-47).

David is speaking with boldness, with indignation at the insult cast upon God's chosen people, and with absolute confidence in God's intention to defeat the Philistine threat. Why is David in his boldness so much fiercer than all of the rest of Israel's army? Why this concern for the dignity of Israel? How does he know that the battle is the Lord's? It is all in the anointing. It is all in the prophetic words spoken over him, fixing his destiny. David has seized the word, believed the word, and is now taking his first step into the words pronounced by Samuel.

A New Man

We know the story, David rushes forward and strikes the Philistine down with a sling stone. He then proceeds to take Goliath's own sword and behead him. The Philistine army is thunderstruck and has lost all courage. They turn to run, while the army of Israel suddenly rises with fresh courage and descends upon them winning a great victory.

David is no longer a shepherd boy. He has become a leader of men. I imagine that this situation is similar to that of the person with a well thought out plan that can quickly control a meeting. So too, a person whose destiny is matched to them can quickly begin to see the vision and become the embodiment of that destiny. The vision that God has planted in David's heart has turned him into a person who influences everyone around him. This forgotten shepherd boy has become the most significant leader in the history of Israel. God, through the prophet Samuel, has matched heaven's desire with the young man David. He is well prepared to begin. He has spent countless hours braving the weather, wild animals and loneliness. He has spent countless hours talking to God, worshiping God, and learning the heart of heaven. David is ready for phase two of his training.

It is important to remember that this destiny is from heaven. David doesn't see it, Samuel doesn't see it, David's family definitely doesn't see it, but God sees it. God saw it in Saul, but Saul failed to step into the role heaven intended for him. God's trust in David has given him the push. Now David is stepping into the vision, the heart of heaven is being released with every step. It will be fifteen years before he becomes king of the southern kingdom Judah. David is beginning to see the world differently and to act differently. Like a fine steel blade, he will find himself heated, hammered and suddenly cooled many times before he becomes the man after God's own heart.

22. David in the Wilderness

Discussion Points:

1. How has David's God-given destiny changed the direction of his life?

2. God has chosen David and matched him to heaven's desire. How does this change David's life?

3. Destiny is re-direction, not an accomplishment. How do we see this in David's life, even when he doesn't appear to be anywhere close to his life to come?

Application:

1. The anointing that David has on his life gives him an indignation and a boldness in facing down Goliath. Has your relationship with God changed you? Do you see things differently now? Do you react differently in your emotions now?

2. It is easy in retrospect, to see how many of the things in David's life were preparing him for his role as king. We can also see that the way that David reacts to his circumstances increases his ability to wear the mantle of God's anointed king of Israel well. Does God have a special desire for you? How might that affect your life going forward?

3. Destiny is re-direction, not an accomplishment. David steps into his God-given role by his attitudes and courage in standing for the heart of God. What sort of destiny do you think that God has for you personally? How might that change your attitudes and behaviors?

24. David in the Wilderness

CHAPTER 3: FLEEING TO NOB & GATH

> The women sang as they played, and said, "Saul has slain his thousands, And David his ten thousands." (1Samuel 18:7).

David's Self-Worth

With the head of Goliath in his hand David is no longer ignored. Saul takes him into his service and will not let him return home (1 Samuel 18:2). David becomes best friends with Jonathan the son of Saul so that they made a covenant with each other and David went out to battle wearing Jonathan's armor (1 Samuel 18:3-4). David was successful at everything Saul sent him to do, so that Saul sets him as a general over his armies (1 Samuel 18:5). David was greatly admired and beloved by the people (1 Samuel 18:7). Possibly for the first time in his life, David is admired and respected, he is in an important position and he is excelling.

David is extremely loyal to Saul, even when Saul is trying to kill him, which is about to happen. Perhaps he saw Saul's respect for him as the respect of a father, since it appears that his own father was a poor representative of fatherhood. David becomes a very close friend of Jonathan, Saul's son and heir apparent, so it is possible that he felt that he now had a real family.

Part of the promise to the man who slays Goliath was the hand of Saul daughter in marriage (1 Samuel 17:25). Saul suggests that David marry Merab his oldest daughter, but David balks, saying, "Who am I, and what is my life or my father's family in Israel, that I should be the king's son-in-law?" (1 Samuel 18:18). It is worth noting that this is at a time when David's reputation is becoming such that Saul is becoming jealous of David. He is secretly hoping to entice David into recklessness that will get him killed.

Saul then changes his mind and marries Merab off to another man (1 Samuel 18:19). Later Saul will have his servants suggest David marry Michal, Saul's younger daughter. Again, David replies, "Is it trivial in your sight to become the king's son-in-law, since I am a poor man and lightly esteemed?" (1 Samuel 18:23).

Despite the fact that David is highly esteemed in Israel, to the point that king Saul himself is murderously jealous of him, David see himself as a poor and lightly esteemed man.

Destiny Derailed

Just when you think nothing can go wrong, things do go horribly wrong. The reason is Saul. As Saul and David are returning from a successful campaign against the Philistines, the women come out to greet them. They sing and dance with joy singing, "Saul has slain his thousands, and David his ten thousands." (1 Samuel 18:7). Unfortunately, Saul was a very self-conscious king. Moreover, he lived in a time when palace coups were common. He feared David and was jealous of David's reputation. The Bible tells us:

Then Saul became very angry, for this saying displeased him; and he said, "They have ascribed to David ten thousands, but to me they have ascribed thousands. Now what more can he have but the kingdom?" Saul looked at David with suspicion from that day on.

Now it came about on the next day that an evil spirit from God came mightily upon Saul, and he raved in the midst of the house, while David was playing the harp with his hand, as usual; and a spear was in Saul's hand. Saul hurled the spear for he thought, "I will pin David to the wall." But David escaped from his presence twice. Now Saul was afraid of David, for the LORD was with him but had departed from Saul. (1 Samuel 18:8-12).

In a moment, through no fault of his own, David goes from being the king's favorite to being the king's dangerous opponent. David respects Saul and does his best to show it, but it is no use.

Unfortunately for Saul, everyone loved David. He was a very successful military leader. Whatever he did, he seemed to prosper. If Saul is going to get rid of David, he has to be cunning.

As it turns out, Saul's daughter Michal loves David. Saul is thinking that he can induce David into reckless battle with the Philistines and get him killed by promising Michal's hand in marriage for a dowry of a hundred foreskins of the Philistines (1 Samuel 18:20-25). David is too good a warrior. David brings 200 foreskins to Saul, so Saul has no choice but allow David to marry Michal (1 Samuel 18:27). David continues to be successful and Saul gets more fearful and jealous until he begins to encourage the murder of David (1 Samuel 19:1). In the end, David has no choice but to flee. Both Jonathan, Saul's son and heir apparent, and Michal, Saul's daughter and David's wife aid David in escaping.

David doesn't have any idea of where to go, so he goes to the place that seems the most sensible, to Samuel. Saul sends men to chase David down. Three squadrons come under the power of the Spirit in Samuel's presence and begin to prophecy until Saul himself comes and immediately goes under the power of the Spirit (1 Samuel 19:18-24).

David goes back to his true friend Jonathan. David is having a hard time believing that Saul really wants to kill him so Jonathan is given the duty of testing his father one more time. The conclusion is clear, David must flee for his life (1 Samuel 20:1-42). This time he runs to Nob where there are a large number of priests (1 Samuel 21:1).

Now let us slow down and notice two things. Most of us jump easily to the belief that so-and-so doesn't like us and wants to do us harm. David is the opposite. Saul has tried to kill him several times, but David still can't believe it. Secondly, when things go badly, David looks for the men of God. In the end, all of his nights learning to sing to the hosts of heaven while watching the sheep will have to be his guide.

Ahimelech the priest of Nob is nervous, he has heard rumors, but David assures him that all is well. Ahimelech helps David who then travels on, but not without being spotted by Doeg the Edomite who runs to tell Saul he has seen David at Nob.

This will cause a problem which David doesn't see as yet. It doesn't occur to David that anyone would kill priests. David figures that if he hides out in Gath, a large Philistine city state, no will know him and Israelites are unlikely to be traveling to Philistine territory, Saul most particularly. Unfortunately, one of the servants of Achish the king of Gath recognizes David. The servants call David "king of the land" and know well the song of the women of Israel "Saul has struck down his thousands, and David his ten thousands" (1 Samuel 21:11). David seems to have leapt from the frying pan into the fire. Thinking quickly David feigns madness (1 Samuel 21:13). The ruse works and Achish has David ushered out (1 Samuel 21:14-15). David escapes back to Israel.

The Heart of David

The psalm that captures the emotions of David's capture and release at Gath is Psalm 56. According to the superscript above the psalm it was written just after the event:

> They stir up strife, they lurk; they watch
> my steps, as they have waited for my
> life. For their crime will they escape? In
> wrath cast down the peoples, O God!
> You have kept count of my tossings;
> put my tears in your bottle. Are they not
> in your book?" (Psalm 56:6-8).

Here it is easy to sense David's fear, how hunted he feels. You can also see bitterness to those who have betrayed him. Oddly he never seems to direct bitterness against Saul. He shakes off all of his negative emotions to praise God and to say thank you for saving me. He doesn't for an instant imagine that his own cunning has saved his neck:

> In God, whose word I praise, in the LORD, whose word I praise, in God I trust; I shall not be afraid. What can man do to me? I must perform my vows to you, O God; I will render thank offerings to you. For you have delivered my soul from death, yes, my feet from falling, that I may walk before God in the light of life" (Psalm 56:10-13).

Psalm 34 is also tagged as commemorating the same events. In this one the fear and the anger have subsided. Instead it rings a jubilant tone from the start:

> I will bless the LORD at all times; his praise shall continually be in my mouth. My soul makes its boast in the LORD; let the humble hear and be glad. Oh, magnify the LORD with me, and let us exalt his name together! I sought the LORD, and he answered me and delivered me from all my fears." (Psalm 34:1-4).

David escapes to the cave of Adullam. Here he hears the ugly news, which we can read in 1 Samuel Chapter 22, Doeg the

Edomite informs Saul that David had received help from the priests of Nob. Saul calls them before him and confronts them. Of course, they have little to say since they didn't know that Saul was chasing David at the time. Never-the-less, Saul commands the guards to slay the priests, but they refuse (1 Samuel 22:17). Doeg then obliges Saul by killing 85 priests that day and he continued on to Nob where he killed men, women, children, even the livestock (1 Samuel 22:18-19). David is crushed. Abiathar one of the sons of Ahimelech and a priest has escaped to David. David mourns, "I have occasioned the death of all the persons of your father's house." (1 Samuel 22:22).

Psalm 52 shows the contempt that David has for Doeg and his actions. He contrasts Doeg's attitude with that of a godly man, describes the results:

> Your tongue plots destruction, like a sharp razor, you worker of deceit. You love evil more than good, and lying more than speaking what is right (Psalm 52:2-3).

> God will break you down forever (Psalm 52:5).

> The righteous shall see and fear, and shall laugh at him, saying, "See the man who would not make God his refuge, but trusted in the abundance of his riches and sought refuge in his own destruction!" But I am like a green olive tree in the house of God. I trust in the

steadfast love of God forever and ever
(Psalm 52:6-8).

Discussion Points:

1. David prefers to think well of everyone. Why is he so angry with Doeg the Edomite, but not with Saul?

2. What is David's relationship with the men of God such as Samuel and the priests of Nob?

3. David is willing to speak out his emotions, good and bad. Why should his fear and anger be part of the Psalms?

4. Why does David feel so guilty in the death of the priests of Nob?

Application:

1. We see that David preferred to think well of people, even when they behaved badly. How do you think of people generally?

2. We see that David was highly incensed at the murder of the priests of Nob. He blamed Doeg the Edomite, who brought the bad report to Saul, and then carried out the sentence when Saul's own guards would not. Still, David did not speak ill of Saul, even though it was Saul who ordered the murder of the priests. Are there people you are angry with? Why? Are there people you should be angry with, but are not? Why?

3. David was surrounded by many people who were not of the highest social standing. He didn't have a lot of choice in who came to follow him. Never-the-less, he did have his mighty men, and he had Abiathar, his priest. Who do you like to hang out with the most? Do they strengthen you or weaken you? When things get difficult, do you go to a different set of people?

4. David went to Nob never dreaming that his visit there would cause the death of all of the priests as well as their families. And yet, when Abiathar comes to him explaining what has happened, David seems genuinely contrite. He feels that the guilt is his. Are there

things in your life, for which you feel guilty, even though you had little control over the situation?

36. David in the Wilderness

CHAPTER 4: IN THE WILDERNESS

> And everyone who was in distress, and everyone who was in debt, and everyone who was bitter in soul, gathered to him. And he became commander over them. And there were with him about four hundred men (1 Samuel 22:2).

Keilah and the Philistines

Since hiding in Philistine territory proved nearly fatal, David returns to Israel. He goes to hide in "the cave of Adullam" (1 Samuel 22:1). There is considerable debate as to where this cave was, (the Hebrew could also imply a stronghold). Some say near Bethlehem as chapter 23 of 2 Samuel (2 Samuel 23:13-17; also 1 Chronicles 11:15-19) relates the story of three of his strong men breaking through Philistine lines to collect water there. Most would place location south of Jerusalem. There is a 'Tel (or hill) Adullam' overlooking the West Bank about fifteen miles south of Jerusalem. Word got out that David was there, so many people gathered to him. Some were mighty warriors who had served under him, his family came, but also many who were angry or bitter, many who were fleeing debt burdens in a day when bankruptcy was not an option. His company swelled to four-hundred men, not including women and children. Before he would return from the wilderness, he would be leading six hundred men.

First things first. Despite questionable relationships with in his natural family, David is careful to take care of his mother and father, taking them to Mizpeh and placing them under the protection of the King of Moab (1 Samuel 22:3-4), we assume for a fee. The prophet Gad comes to David and warns him to flee (1 Samuel 22:5), so David begins his wilderness trials fleeing from place to place, just trying to stay one step ahead of Saul. At the same time David is attempting to protect many who are simply fleeing the fate of the priests of Nob. His force is not large enough to confront Saul, nor is it David's desire to confront Saul. But with hundreds of mouths to feed, it is difficult for David to hide for long.

As if that is not enough, news comes to him: "the Philistines are fighting against Keilah and are plundering the threshing floors" (1 Samuel 23:1). He could have said, Saul is the king, he needs to take care of that issue. David asks God, "Shall I go and attack these Philistines?" (1 Samuel 23:2). His men were already in fear of Saul, but to take their small force and intentionally attack a Philistine army seems foolish to them. They balk at David's suggestion. David inquires again, and God says, "Arise, go down to Keilah, for I will give the Philistines into your hand." (1 Samuel 23:4).

There are several things that this passage makes clear. First is that David has a genuine concern for the people of Israel. His care for his people outweighs his concern for self-preservation. And, he immediately asks God for direction. When his men object, David asks God for confirmation. With that confirmation, he acts decisively. David and his small army route the Philistines and save Keilah (1 Samuel 23:5). Afterwards, David seeks God's council again and realizes that he must flee Keilah.

The Negeb

David flees deeper into the Negeb, a barren land in the southern part of Israel. Here there are few trees, and food and water are scarce. Moreover, raiding parties from neighboring tribes are frequent here. In the Negeb, David will begin to feel the full weight of his exile:

> Look to the right and see: there is none who takes notice of me; no refuge remains to me; no one cares for my soul. I cry to you, O LORD; I say, "You are my refuge, my portion in the land of the living." Attend to my cry, for I am brought very low! Deliver me from my persecutors, for they are too strong for me! (Psalm 142:4-6).

So, David's prayer rings out from "when he was in the cave" (Psalm 142:1).

David is not relying on any schemes he might concoct. He is declaring, "You [God] are my refuge (Psalm 142:5). Psalm 63, written "when he was in the wilderness of Judah" (Psalm 63:1), clearly displays the longing of David's heart. It has become a favorite contemporary worship song. If we look at the circumstances in which David wrote this psalm, we will notice an intensity in it that the lyric beauty of the psalm tends to mask:

> *A Psalm of David, when he was in the wilderness of Judah.*
>
> O God, You are my God; I shall seek You earnestly; My soul thirsts for You, my flesh yearns for You, In a dry and weary land where there is no water.
>
> Thus I have seen You in the sanctuary, To see Your power and Your glory.
>
> Because Your lovingkindness is better than life, My lips will praise You.
>
> So I will bless You as long as I live; I will lift up my hands in Your name.
>
> My soul is satisfied as with marrow and fatness, And my mouth offers praises with joyful lips.
>
> When I remember You on my bed, I meditate on You in the night watches,
>
> For You have been my help, And in the shadow of Your wings I sing for joy.
>
> My soul clings to You; Your right hand upholds me.

But those who seek my life to destroy it,
Will go into the depths of the earth.

They will be delivered over to the
power of the sword; They will be a prey
for foxes.

But the king will rejoice in God; Everyone who swears by Him will glory, For
the mouths of those who speak lies will
be stopped (Psalm 63:1-11).

The first two verses voice an incredible longing for God's presence. This psalm matches Psalm 42 in many ways. That psalm starts with another memorable statement of longing: "As the deer pants for the water brooks, So my soul pants for you, O God. My soul thirsts for God, for the living God" (Psalm 42:1-2). Exiled to the Negeb, thirst seems to be an apt metaphor for his desperate situation. While most of us tend to ruminate Job-like for seeming ages, David follows the flow upward: "I have seen you". "I have seen "your power and your glory". "My lips will praise you" (Psalm 63:2-4). And so David launches into several verses of the most magnificent praise. In Psalm 42, the psalmist stops the flow to ask, "Why are you in despair, O my soul? And why have you become disturbed within me? Hope in God, for I shall again praise Him For the help of His presence. O my God, my soul is in despair within me; Therefore I remember You from the land of the Jordan And the peaks of Hermon, from Mount Mizar" (Psalm 42:5-6). David moves effortlessly between ruminating on his struggles and reaching upwards in praise. The psalm sweeps us right along with him.

David continues to move higher in his devotions, he sees his own deliverance from woe: "My soul will be satisfied as with marrow and fatness" (Psalm 63:5). This is no prosperity gospel, his vision is based on the firm foundation of his relationship with God, which is a tried and tested relationship. David is confident of God's help. He states, "You have been my help" (Psalm 63:7).

What we are seeing at work is David with a tried and true formula for overcoming the darkness from without that is trying to work its way into his soul. I doubt he ever wrote it out as his five points to spiritual fitness. Rather this is a pattern that slipped under his skin on many lonely nights when the cold and dark pressed about him, whispering rejection. He would pull out his harp and play a song for the LORD. Psalm 57, also written "when he fled from Saul in the cave" (Psalm 57:1), exposes the warfare underneath. "Be gracious to me, O God, be gracious to me, For my soul takes refuge in You" (Psalm 57:1). He begins, "I will cry to God Most High, To God who accomplishes all things for me" (Psalm 57:2). His gaze upwards allows him to shift into confident declaration: "He will send from heaven and save me" (Psalm 57:3). The psalm struggles back and forth: "My soul is among lions" (Psalm 57:4). "Be exalted, O God" (Psalm 57:5). "They have prepared a net for my steps" (Psalm 57:6). "They themselves have fallen into the midst of it" (Psalm 57:6). "My heart is steadfast, O God" (Psalm 57:7). And then we see him break through:

> Awake, my glory! Awake, harp and
> lyre! I will awaken the dawn! I will give

thanks to you, O Lord, among the peoples; I will sing praises to you among
the nations. For your lovingkindness is
great to the heavens, And Your truth to
the clouds. Be exalted above the heavens, O God! Let your glory be above all
the earth! (Psalm 57:8-11).

By this process of internal warfare, external praise, and remembering all the good that God has done for him so far,
David is able to stir his soul so that he clearly sees his enemies
defeated, as he sees God's care for him, "But the king will
rejoice in God; Everyone who swears by Him will glory, For
the mouths of those who speak lies will be stopped." (Psalm
63:11). At this point, I do not believe that David is affirming
a creed or "standing on the word." He is declaring what his
soul sees. It is all a part of his close relationship with God.

44. David in the Wilderness

Discussion Points:

1. How is David's heart and/or anointing shown in his defense of Keilah?

2. Where does David go for advice?

3. When David's men object out of fear, how does David deal with their fear?

4. Seeing Psalm 63 in the light of the circumstances David was under, how does that change your understanding of it?

5. Who is David's closest friend in the wilderness?

Application:

1. Sometimes we feel prompted to do something, but we don't necessarily know why. Perhaps, the urgency doesn't seem to come from us naturally. Is it possible that these are moments when the Holy Spirit is prompting you? Think of a situation in your life that shows God's heart at work in and through you? These may be small acts or big ones.

2. We see that David went to Samuel the prophet at first. When he had to leave there, he went to the priests of Nob. But finally, he found himself in the Philistine city of Gath where he had no one to rely on except God? As he fled to the Negeb, he had many people gathering around him, but few wise councilors. Where do you go for advice?

3. In so many of the psalms, we see that David is afraid and oppressed. We see him reaching out to God for help, for direction, as well as for emotional support. Listening to the nightly news can stir up fear, if we don't have enough difficulty in our lives to stir it up already. How do you deal with fear? When people around you are afraid, are you able to calm them?

4. We see that David overcomes his fears many times, by simply praising God. Even though his circumstances haven't changed, his mood had radically altered from one of anxiety to one of jubilance. Are you able to praise God in difficult circumstances?

CHAPTER 5: SAUL'S LIFE

> David said to Saul, "Why do you listen
> to the words of men, saying, 'Behold,
> David seeks to harm you?' Behold,
> this day your eyes have seen that the
> LORD had given you today into my
> hand in the cave, and some said to
> kill you, but my eye had pity on you;
> and I said, 'I will not stretch out my
> hand against my lord, for he is the
> LORD'S anointed'" (1 Samuel 24:9-10).

Potty Break

David spares Saul's life, not once, but twice (1 Samuel chapter 24 & 26). In chapter 24, Saul, who is pursuing David to kill him, enters a cave to relieve himself. He is alone and therefore quite vulnerable. He is unaware that David and his men are hiding in this very cave (1Samuel 24:3). His men press David with his own words "Here is the day of which the LORD said to you, 'Behold, I will give your enemy into your hand, and you shall do to him as it shall seem good to you'" (1Samuel 24:4).

A couple of things to remember here: God has never said He would give Saul into David's hand, and David has never asked for it. David's men, moreover, are not the cream of Israel's crop. Most of them have come to David out of desperation owing to financial or legal problems. They are tempted by a possible quick end to their problems. I sense that David is listening for God's voice. When he doesn't hear it, he is cautious.

David is in a dark and desperate place. He is not being opposed, he is being hunted down, pursued with one purpose in mind: the death of David. Psalm 54, composed, according to the script at the top, when the Ziphites had informed Saul of David's location in the Negeb, concludes: "For He has delivered me from all trouble, And my eye has looked with satisfaction upon my enemies" (Psalm 54:7). This could be what the men are referring to above. But, as mentioned it does not give David permission to kill Saul. Of his adversaries, David says, "For strangers have risen against me And violent men have sought my life; They have not set God before them" (Psalm 54:3).

In Psalm 143, a psalm of David, but not directly attached to a specific event, David says, "You will cut off my enemies" in the ESV. However, the NASB, states it more as a request, "in Your lovingkindness, cut off my enemies" (Psalm 143:12). This psalm does speak of sitting in darkness, which in the circumstances of the En Gedi cave where David is sitting in the above account. He says, "the enemy has persecuted my soul" (Psalm 143:3). David clearly realizes that not only is his life in danger, but all of his thoughts and feelings are being pushed towards darkness.

Remember

The most remarkable aspect of David's personality is his ability to continually free his thoughts from the world in front of him and to look for God, both in past victories over tremendous difficulties and in promises and prophecies. It is this aspect of David's personality that makes him a true leader loved by God. In the midst of very difficult circumstances, David is able see God's path ahead of him, and refuse to deviate from it, not even for a prophetic word repackaged to fit the needs of the moment.

> I remember the days of old; I meditate
> on all Your doings; I muse on the work
> of Your hands (Psalm 143:5).

Although Psalm 143 doesn't specify which past events he is thinking about, David is telling God, in this psalm/prayer, 'I remember'. Is David remembering how the towering giant Goliath fell before him? One stone found its mark, while Goliath stood still mocking the boy. Or is David remembering how he eluded Saul's spear on more than one occasion? Why did King Achish let David go? How is it that in the moment that David was being pinned down in the wilderness of Ziph that Saul suddenly had to pull away to stop a Philistine attack? Search the word 'remember' in the Psalms, it is a theme which comes up again and again.

God's covenant is celebrated in what He has done. In this way, we can trust in our hope of what He will do. The future is informed by the past. We see this in the celebration of the first Passover celebration: "Moses said to the people, 'Remember this day in which you went out from Egypt, from the house of slavery; for by a powerful hand the LORD brought you out from this place.'" (Exodus 13:3). When Jesus was about to face capture and a torturous death, he sits down to eat: "when He had taken some bread and given thanks, He broke it and gave it to them, saying, 'This is My body which is given for you; do this in remembrance of Me'" (Luke 22:19). The promises are made concrete not by our imagination, but by remembering what has already been done for us.

The Passover or the Eucharist bread and wine are large scale covenant celebrations. Within these larger covenants are the individual relationships with God. Every Jew and every Christian has the ability to draw near to God. How? Calling on God in prayer and fasting. Finding God's heart in the Bible and in putting into practice the actions which win God's heart: mercy, kindness, justice and so on. Resisting the voices, loud and many, to compromise, try a little perversion, a little rebellion, do your own thing. In this way, small miracles begin to pile up. Someone is strengthened who had no hope. A life is changed. A catastrophe is averted. Peace comes in a fearful situation. Whatever happens, notice when God shows up, and remember. Remember that God hears you, and God responds. God has a relationship with the body of Christ, with godly nations, but God also has a relationship with every living soul that has breath, and that means you. Covet that relationship and deepen it, by personal interaction and by remembrance. This is what we see David doing time and time again.

> Let me hear in the morning of your steadfast love, for in you I trust. Make me know the way I should go, for to you I lift up my soul (Psalm 143:8).

David is not remembering the bad times or the things that have been said or done against him. These do not lift him up and encourage him. He is not remembering the adversary's hand; he is remembering God's hand in his life.

The second encouragement that David has is that several prophecies have been spoken over him. First, he was anointed by Samuel (1 Samuel 16:12-13). The meaning was clear. When God tells him to go, Samuel protests, "Saul will kill me" (1 Samuel 16:2). Samuel goes under the pretense of making a sacrifice (1 Samuel 16:3-5). He anoints David in front of his family alone and quickly leaves (1 Samuel 16:13). The need for secrecy and the fear surrounding Samuel's visit shows that this was not a simple 'impartation'. It says that "the Spirit of the LORD rushed upon David from that day forward" (1 Samuel 16:13). David's awareness of God, and of his own destiny in God were magnified from that day forward.

Most remarkable is that Jonathan, the son of King Saul and the heir apparent, knows that God is with David. He has already made a covenant with David because of it: "You shall not cut off your lovingkindness from my house forever, not even when the LORD cuts off every one of the enemies of David from the face of the earth" (1 Samuel 20:15). Jonathan comes to David in the wilderness and "encouraged him [David] in God" (1 Samuel 23:16). How? Jonathan prophesies over David, "Do not be afraid, because the hand of Saul my father will not find you, and you will be king over Israel and I will be next to you; and Saul my father knows that also" (1 Samuel 23:17). Jonathan, as heir apparent, would not be disposed to believing that David would be the next king. But he does and comes to David to pledge his support.

So here is David: he is running and hiding in a barren inhospitable land with little food or water. He has a band of six-hundred misfits and social rejects. Pursuing him is a well-trained, well-armed, and a well-supplied army of three thousand chosen men who have lookouts everywhere. His situation looks hopeless. On the other hand, he knows that God has been protecting him, and further, he has every reason to believe that God wants to make him king over Israel. In this dilemma, suddenly David finds Saul right in front of him, inches from the tip of his blade, caught literally with his pants down (1 Samuel 24:3).

Does he put an end to Saul right now? Jonathan, Saul's son, has said the "LORD cuts off every one of the enemies of David", and all his men know that God's word to David is that, "Behold; I am about to give your enemy into your hand, and you shall do to him as it seems good to you" (1 Samuel 24:4). Saul is definitely an enemy to David. Why should David hesitate?

There is only one explanation, it doesn't feel right. In the midst of this highly charged moment, David pauses and breathes, "Answer me quickly, O LORD! My spirit fails!" (Psalm 143:7). He rises and quietly cuts off the edge of Saul's robe (1 Samuel 24:4). He has promised himself to Saul, and even now refuses to betray that trust.

This event runs parallel to Samuel's prophecy over Saul. Because of Saul's disobedience to the word of the LORD, Samuel prophecies that Saul has been rejected by God. When Samuel turns to leave, Saul grabs Samuel's robe and it tears.

Samuel prophecies, "The LORD has torn the kingdom of Israel from you today and has given it to your neighbor, who is better than you" (1 Samuel 15:28).

When Saul and his army have moved away some distance, David stands on a bluff holding the edge of Saul's robe, displaying his lack of ill-will towards Saul. Saul replies, "Is this your voice, my son David?" And Saul, it says, lifted up his voice and wept. He said to David, "You are more righteous than I; for you have dealt well with me, while I have dealt wickedly with you.

> You have declared today that you have done good to me, that the LORD delivered me into your hand and yet you did not kill me. For if a man finds his enemy, will he let him go away safely? May the LORD therefore reward you with good in return for what you have done to me this day. Now, behold, I know that you will surely be king, and that the kingdom of Israel will be established in your hand. So now swear to me by the LORD that you will not cut off my descendants after me and that you will not destroy my name from my father's household" (1 Samuel 24:18-21).

A Deep Sleep

Saul does not keep his word. He is soon back pursuing David. In an even more remarkable way, the scene from En Gedi repeats itself. David and two men approach Saul's army at night. All three thousand men are in a deep sleep, which allows David to walk into the camp right up to where Saul lies sleeping. His friend Abishai tells David, "Today God has delivered your enemy into your hand; now therefore, please let me strike him with the spear to the ground with one stroke, and I will not strike him the second time" (1 Samuel 26:8). David is immediate in his reply, "Do not destroy him, for who can stretch out his hand against the LORD'S anointed and be without guilt?" (1 Samuel 26:9). David continues, "As the LORD lives, surely the LORD will strike him, or his day will come that he dies, or he will go down into battle and perish. The LORD forbid that I should stretch out my hand against the LORD'S anointed; but now please take the spear that is at his head and the jug of water, and let us go" (1 Samuel 26:10-11). Since the last encounter, David has had time to mull over his response and is now quick and decisive. He knows his answer ahead of time.

Discussion Points:

1. How does David show his value for God's anointing?

2. Why does David refuse to take things in his own hands?

3. How do we see David rely on the LORD?

4. What are the promises of God that David can rely upon?

Application:

1. David had a clear word over his life from the prophet Samuel. Moreover, Samuel's anointing and prayer over him changed his personality to a more expansive compassion for God's people. Few of us have such dramatic anointings, but everyone that God brings into His kingdom has a place reserved for them. Do you recognize God's hand on you in your life? Have you done anything to nurture it and help it grow?

2. We see that David had the temptation to take things into his own hands and kill Saul. He has the foresight to resist the temptation. Are you tempted to take things into your own hands at times? Think of a specific incidence. How did you react? How do you think you can you rely on the LORD more?

3. When you look back over your life, are there times that you can see God was at work on your behalf? Are there moments that you can remember of a special closeness with God? Do you think to recall those memories in times of difficult circumstances?

4. David had many times when those around him have affirmed his destiny. These were words of promise that God was at work despite his apparent circum-

stances. David could encourage himself by remembering these words spoken over him. Are there trusted people in your life who have spoken words over you that you can use to remember and encourage yourself in difficult times? Are there promises of God for you, that you can rely upon?

58. David in the Wilderness

CHAPTER 6: WISE COUNSEL

> And when the LORD does for my lord according to all the good that He has spoken concerning you, and appoints you ruler over Israel, this will not cause grief or a troubled heart to my lord, both by having shed blood without cause and by my lord having avenged himself. When the LORD deals well with my lord, then remember your maidservant (1 Samuel 25:30-31).

A Wise Woman

We have already seen that David was surrounded by social rejects, misfits, criminals and debtors. Their counsel was not trustworthy. David relied on his prayers to God, as well as inquiries to the ephod that Ahimelech had brought when he fled Saul (1 Samuel 23:6 & 9-12). But David was a man of action. He occasionally went into action before he had stopped to think through the results or to inquire of the LORD. This is abundantly clear in the incident in the wilderness with Nabal and Abigail.

In First Samuel, Chapter 25, the story unfolds: David, besides running from Saul, has also been protecting the settlements in the wilderness of Judah, the Negeb. It was the time of sheep shearing and David heard that a very wealthy man by the name of Nabal was shearing sheep with his men. David sent some of his young men to ask for food from Nabal (1 Samuel 25:5-9). "Nabal answered David's servants and said, 'Who is David? And who is the son of Jesse? There are many servants today who are each breaking away from his master. Shall I then take my bread and my water and my meat that I have slaughtered for my shearers, and give it to men whose origin I do not know?'" (1 Samuel 25:10-11). Nabal accused David of rebellion, which is untrue, and unwisely insulted a man with an army of 600 men. Even if David's men are largely misfits, they are now a seasoned fighting force. Moreover, there are several exceptional warriors with him, David's mighty men (1 Chronicles 11:10-47).

When Nabal's reply is relayed to David, his answer is quick: "Each of you gird on his sword" (1 Samuel 25:13). David and 400 men march towards Nabal's encampment. Nabal's servants know that this will not end well for them and so they tell the situation to Abigail, Nabal's wife. "Behold, David sent messengers from the wilderness to greet our master, and he scorned them. Yet the men were very good to us, and we were not insulted, nor did we miss anything as long as we went about with them, while we were in the fields. They were a wall to us both by night and by day, all the time we were with them tending the sheep. Now therefore, know and consider what you should do, for evil is plotted against our master and against all his household; and he is such a worthless man that no one can speak to him" (1 Samuel 25:14-17).

Abigail immediately loads a large store of provisions on donkeys and sends servants ahead to announce her coming. She, herself, comes with the gift. David is steamed to say the least: "Surely in vain I have guarded all that this man has in the wilderness, so that nothing was missed of all that belonged to him; and he has returned me evil for good. May God do so to the enemies of David, and more also, if by morning I leave as much as one male of any who belong to him." (1 Samuel 25:21-22).

Abigail arrives and gets down from her donkey, she bows low before David, she begins to apologize and to reason with David:

> On me alone, my lord, be the blame. And please let your maidservant speak to you, and listen to the words of your maidservant. Please do not let my lord pay attention to this worthless man, Nabal, for as his name is, so is he. Nabal is his name and folly is with him; but I your maidservant did not see the young men of my lord whom you sent. Now therefore, my lord, as the LORD lives, and as your soul lives, since the LORD has restrained you from shedding blood, and from avenging yourself by your own hand, now then let your enemies and those who seek evil against my lord, be as Nabal. Now let this gift which your maidservant has brought to my lord be given to the young men who accompany my lord. Please forgive the transgression of your maidservant; for the LORD will certainly make for my

lord an enduring house, because my lord is fighting the battles of the LORD, and evil will not be found in you all your days. Should anyone rise up to pursue you and to seek your life, then the life of my lord shall be bound in the bundle of the living with the LORD your God; but the lives of your enemies He will sling out as from the hollow of a sling. And when the LORD does for my lord according to all the good that He has spoken concerning you, and appoints you ruler over Israel, this will not cause grief or a troubled heart to my lord, both by having shed blood without cause and by my lord having avenged himself. When the LORD deals well with my lord, then remember your maidservant (1 Samuel 25:24-31).

David hears Abigail's plea. He immediately recognizes that she speaks with great wisdom. It's as if the recently departed prophet Samuel had come back to life to give him counsel. "Blessed be the LORD God of Israel, who sent you this day to meet me, and blessed be your discernment, and blessed be you, who have kept me this day from bloodshed and from avenging myself by my own hand. Nevertheless, as the LORD God of Israel lives, who has restrained me from harming you, unless you had come quickly to meet me, surely there would not have been left to Nabal until the morning light as much as one male" (1 Samuel 25:32-34). He receives Abigail's gift and turns his troop around.

It does not end well for Nabal. When Abigail returns to tell him what has transpired, Nabal is inebriated so she waits. When she tells him the next day, Nabal is in shock, literally. "But in the morning, when the wine had gone out of Nabal, his wife told him these things, and his heart died within him so that he became as a stone" (1 Samuel 25:37). Ten days later he dies. "When David heard that Nabal was dead, he said, 'Blessed be the LORD, who has pleaded the cause of my reproach from the hand of Nabal and has kept back His servant from evil. The LORD has also returned the evildoing of Nabal on his own head.' Then David sent a proposal to Abigail, to take her as his wife" (1 Samuel 25:39).

So, Abigail becomes David's wife. Now stop and think about this situation. David is worked up emotionally and with hundreds of men in his company he sets out to remove his reproach. But he is met by a woman who convinces him that he is on the wrong track. He changes his mind and withdraws. David is living in a patriarchal society, and he, the leader, has been stopped in his tracks by a woman. He recognizes the wisdom in Abigail's argument, and humbles himself to it. With 600 pairs of eyes on him, David says thank you for stopping me. The men could let that pass, since they did get a large peace offering. Myself, when confronted, I think I would have difficulty humbling myself if there was only one witness. David goes beyond that; he takes this woman as his wife. How do his men reconcile this in their minds? Has she beguiled him?

A Love of Wisdom

Looking over the life of David, we notice several things which are at work here. One is that David is not particularly concerned with his image. He seems to be unaware of just how highly those around him think of him. What is important is his relationship with God. And he knows that his worship will bring respect from God's people. Notice his answer to Michal, Saul's daughter who sneers at his "shameless" dancing before the LORD: "I will celebrate before the LORD. I will be more lightly esteemed than this and will be humble in my own eyes, but with the maids of whom you have spoken, with them I will be distinguished" (2 Samuel 6:20-22).

Secondly, David respects wise counsel and keeps wise advisors around him. When David flees from the rebellion of his own son Absalom, it is told to him that a particular counselor Ahithophel has gone over to the rebellion. David prays, "O LORD, I pray, make the counsel of Ahithophel foolishness" (2 Samuel 15:31). Cleverly, David sends his loyal friend and counselor, Hushai the Archite to subvert the counsel of Ahithophel (2 Samuel 15:34). Oddly, this rebellion was facilitated when David listened to the counsel of a "wise woman of Tekoa", who is put to the task by Joab, resulting in Absalom's restoration to royal privilege (2 Samuel 14:1-21). Hindsight being 20-20, the counsel seems to have been unwise. The important point is that David keeps wise and godly men and women around him intentionally.

And finally, David's respect for truth before God causes him to humble himself before Nathan the prophet when he is confronted over his sin regarding Bathsheba. When Samuel had a word of rebuke for Saul, he had to leave Saul's presence (1 Samuel 15:35). When God tells Samuel to go and anoint David, Samuel protests, "How can I go? When Saul hears of it, he will kill me" (1 Samuel 16:2). It was dangerous to rebuke

Saul. David, on the other hand, welcomed Godly counsel whether it was to his liking or not. Nathan had ready access to David, regardless. In Second Samuel Chapter 12, Nathan appears with a stinging rebuke from the LORD complete with the pronouncement of God's curses (2 Samuel 12:1-12). David doesn't miss a beat. He says, "I have sinned against the LORD" (2 Samuel 12:13). "Create in me a clean heart, O God, And renew a steadfast spirit within me" (Psalm 51:10). This psalm is introduced: "A Psalm of David, when Nathan the prophet came to him, after he had gone in to Bathsheba" according to the superscription above verse 1. The psalm flows with contrition: "Behold, I was brought forth in iniquity, And in sin my mother conceived me" (Psalm 51:5). David understands, "Behold, You desire truth in the innermost being, And in the hidden part You will make me know wisdom" (Psalm 51:6). He has violated the truth set in his inward being and moved against the wisdom set in his heart. David has no quarrel with Nathan, his quarrel is with God, for which he can only ask for mercy. David sees the truth and honors it.

Discussion Points:

1. How difficult was it for David to humble himself to Abigail in front of men?

2. Why did David put such a high priority on having wise councilors around him?

3. How did David remain teachable?

Application:

1. We see David in a situation where Nabal has made
   him murderously angry. Abigail speaks wisdom to
   David, calming him and causing him to humble himself and change course. It would not appear to have
   been easy for David to humble himself at that moment. Think of a time when it was difficult for you to
   humble yourself? How did you do?

2. David immediately recognized that Abigail was a
   wise councilor. When Nabal dies suddenly, David
   takes her as his wife. Later, when David is king, he
   especially values the council of specific men. Do you
   have wise councilors in your life?

3. We see that David is able to be taught by the wife of
   the man he ison his way to murder. We also see that
   Nathan and others are able to speak to him and he
   listens, even when the message is a bitter pill to swal-
   low. He allows good council to shape his life. How
   teachable are you? What attitudes can you cultivate
   to help you to become more teachable?

68. David in the Wilderness

CHAPTER 7: EVERYTHING CHANGES

> He sent from on high, He took me; He drew me out of many waters. He delivered me from my strong enemy, And from those who hated me, for they were too mighty for me. They confronted me in the day of my calamity, But the LORD was my stay. He brought me forth also into a broad place; He rescued me, because He delighted in me (Psalm 18:16-19).

The Darkest Hour

The darkest hour is just before dawn. This old phrase is the perfect description of David's wilderness troubles. David has been in the wilderness running from Saul for more than a decade and there seems to be no let up. He decides, "Now I will perish one day by the hand of Saul. There is nothing better for me than to escape into the land of the Philistines. Saul then will despair of searching for me anymore in all the territory of Israel, and I will escape from his hand" (1 Samuel 27:1). Things are pretty hopeless when the safest place to be is under the protection of Achish, king of Gath, from whom he had fled ten years earlier. But there goes David with his band of men. Achish grants him the town of Ziklag to dwell in (1 Samuel 27:6).

To make his presence palatable to the Philistine king, David convinces him that he is raiding Israelite villages when in fact he is raiding anything but Israelite or Philistine villages (1 Samuel 27:8-12). This becomes a problem when the Philistines decide to make war on Israel (1 Samuel 28:1). David has no choice but to agree to go up to battle alongside Achish against Israel.

As the Philistine troops pass in review before the Philistine commanders, there is David and his 600 men. The commanders were angry with Achish and insisted that David and his men be sent back to Ziklag (1 Samuel 29:3-7). In case David was not feeling insecure enough, now his presence with the Philistines is exposed, his situation is likely to get even more uncomfortable.

But wait, it gets even worse. "Then it happened when David and his men came to Ziklag on the third day, that the Amalekites had made a raid on the Negev and on Ziklag, and had overthrown Ziklag and burned it with fire; and they took captive the women and all who were in it, both small and great, without killing anyone, and carried them off and went their way" (1 Samuel 30:1-2). David's story is starting to look like Job's.

David's misery is compounded when the blame isn't focused on the Amalekites, but on him: "Moreover David was greatly distressed because the people spoke of stoning him, for all the people were embittered, each one because of his sons and his daughters" (1 Samuel 30:6). This is the place for all those cute aphorisms: 'down to zero', 'lower than snail slime', and so on. But imagine the turmoil in his heart. I've been in this sort of turmoil. It's impossible to sleep. I wasn't even able to lie down, I just crouched in the corner all night long. 'Slough of despond' doesn't begin to capture the despair. But...

"But David strengthened himself in the LORD his God" (1 Samuel 30:6). With this short phrase, David rises above his dire circumstance. His relationship with God is so close, that in the midst of earthly desolation, he never feels alone. He has somewhere to go and receive strength and refreshing. The only insight we can get as to what this strengthening might have looked like is from the psalms of David:

> Hear my prayer, O LORD, Give ear to my supplications! Answer me in Your faithfulness, in Your righteousness! And do not enter into judgment with Your servant, For in Your sight no man living is righteous.

> For the enemy has persecuted my soul; He has crushed my life to the ground; He has made me dwell in dark places, like those who have long been dead. Therefore my spirit is overwhelmed within me; My heart is appalled within me.

> I remember the days of old; I meditate on all Your doings; I muse on the work of Your hands. I stretch out my hands to You; My soul longs for You, as a parched land. *Selah.*

> Answer me quickly, O LORD, my spirit fails; Do not hide Your face from

me, Or I will become like those who go down to the pit. Let me hear Your lovingkindness in the morning; For I trust in You; Teach me the way in which I should walk; For to You I lift up my soul. Deliver me, O LORD, from my enemies; I take refuge in You. Teach me to do Your will, For You are my God; Let Your good Spirit lead me on level ground. For the sake of Your name, O LORD, revive me.

In Your righteousness bring my soul out of trouble. And in Your lovingkindness, cut off my enemies And destroy all those who afflict my soul, For I am Your servant (Psalm 143:1-12).

We know that however this strengthening looked, it had the right effect. Immediately David is able to snap into action:

Then David said to Abiathar the priest, the son of Ahimelech, "Please bring me the ephod." So Abiathar brought the ephod to David. David inquired of the LORD, saying, "Shall I pursue this band? Shall I overtake them?" And He said to him, "Pursue, for you will surely overtake them, and you will surely rescue all" (1 Samuel 30:7-8).

Clear thinking and confidence change the desperate atmosphere instantly. Talk of stoning David is shelved. David and all 600 men set out to pursue the Amalekites. They overtake the raiders and decimate them. Every captive is recovered. All of their stolen goods are recovered as well as the plunder from numerous other raids (1 Samuel 30:9-20).

My Misery is Gone

In victory, David does not exalt. One third of the men had been too exhausted to continue on to the final battle. Remember that many of those who follow David are societies least desirable, "wicked and worthless fellows". These men suggest to David, "Because they did not go with us, we will not give them any of the spoil that we have recovered, except to every man his wife and his children, that they may lead them away and depart" (1 Samuel 30:22). David is firm: "You must not do so, my brothers, with what the LORD has given us, who has kept us and delivered into our hand the band that came against us. And who will listen to you in this matter? For as his share is who goes down to the battle, so shall his share be who stays by the baggage; they shall share alike" (1 Samuel 30:23-24).

David is also generous. When he returns to Ziklag, he immediately sends a part of the spoil to the elders of Judah, as well as to all of those towns and cities where he had the occasion to find himself in his times of trouble (1 Samuel 30:26-31).

Saul and Jonathan are not so fortunate. The battle with the Philistines goes badly. Saul and Jonathan are overtaken and killed. On the one hand, this is good news for David. His troubles are over and he is now able to return to Israel. But David seems to ignore that completely. This is bad news for Israel who has been defeated at the hand of the Philistines. Saul and his good friend Jonathan are dead and the Philistine's exalt over their victory. In this account, the Amalekite who has brought the news claims to have killed Saul at Saul's own request (2 Samuel 1:2-13). David is indignant, "How is it you were not afraid to stretch out your hand to destroy the LORD'S anointed?" (2 Samuel 1:14). David orders him to be killed immediately (2 Samuel 1:15).

And so, David laments the fall of Saul and Jonathan as the fall of great warriors fallen in battle. Verses 19 through 27 of Second Samuel contain "The Song of the Bow", David's lament for Saul and Jonathan that he commanded to be taught to all of Judah. "Your beauty, O Israel, is slain on your high places! How have the mighty fallen!" (2 Samuel 1:19).

After inquiring of the LORD, David goes up to Hebron where the men of Judah anoint him king.

Discussion Points:

1. What do you think it looked like when David strengthen himself in God?

2. How difficult must it have been for David to keep from becoming depressed and defeated?

3. How did David change the atmosphere around him, when the men still wanted to stone him?

4. David does not exalt. Why not?

5. After so many years of deprivation, how is David is so generous with his good fortune?

Application:

1. When David seems to have hit rock bottom, he strengthens himself in the Lord. Have you ever felt depressed and defeated? How did you get out of that feeling? Do you know how to strengthen yourself in God? What does that look like for you?

2. The circumstances in which David goes to strengthen himself in the Lord couldn't have been worse. His own men are talking of stoning him. But, after David has his talk with God, he consults Abiathar and gets definite direction from on high. The men immediately fall in behind David. Have you been in places or situations where the atmosphere seemed toxic? Was there anything you could do to change the atmosphere?

3. David has a rag to riches moment almost overnight. He is able to transition from being the hunted rebel, to being the king. In the process, he remains respectful to his former adversary. In fact, he goes to great lengths to honor the memory of Saul. When you have a great breakthrough or win a great honor, how do you act? How do you treat former adversaries who have been defeated?

CHAPTER 8: THE FACE OF GOD

Then it came about afterwards that David inquired of the LORD, saying, "Shall I go up to one of the cities of Judah?" And the LORD said to him, "Go up." So David said, "Where shall I go up?" And He said, "To Hebron." David went up there, and his two wives also, Ahinoam the Jezreelitess and Abigail the widow of Nabal the Carmelite. And David brought up his men who were with him, each with his household; and they lived in the cities of Hebron. Then the men of Judah came and there anointed David king over the house of Judah (2 Samuel 2:1-4).

The King of Judah

It would be good to review and re-examine some of the things which make David the obvious candidate as replacement for Saul. While Saul had spent a great deal of time hunting down his greatest general in order to kill him, David was continually hunting down the raiding parties which plagued Judah. While Saul levied taxes and conscripted young men to harass David, David was quick to share the spoil taken from large raiding parties. David was a continual blessing to Judah even in the midst of his trials. David was a mighty warrior, with a reputation greater than that of Saul. It didn't hurt that David was of the tribe of Judah, whereas Saul was a Benjamite.

It seemed obvious to many people that David was destined to be the king. We hear that from Abigail (1 Samuel 25:30). But more importantly, Jonathan, the heir apparent, encourages David and prophecies that David will be king (1 Samuel 23:17). It is not clear that Samuel's anointing of David was public knowledge, but Samuel's public rebuke of Saul was well known: "The LORD has torn the kingdom of Israel from you today and has given it to your neighbor, who is better than you. Also the Glory of Israel will not lie or change His mind; for He is not a man that He should change His mind" (1 Samuel 15:28-29).

But this is all the view from the world's vantage point. Politics was running in David's favor. Heaven's view also favors David, but for very different reasons. Heaven has anointed David through Samuel as we know. Where Saul used the position to his own advantage, he never cultivated the anointing. David has stepped into that anointing even though he is not yet king. As Abigail states it: "the LORD will certainly make for my lord an enduring house, because my lord is fighting the battles of the LORD, and evil will not be found in you all your days" (1 Samuel 25:28).

We saw that already in the confrontation with Goliath, David's perspective of the situation was very different from any one else around him. He saw the battle as the Lord's battle and the people of Israel as the Lord's people. A threat against

Israel was to challenge God directly. David's personal concerns became small in light of national concerns and especially God's concern. We see this also when the Philistines are attacking Keilah, David's heart is immediately to go and to rescue this town. He inquires of the LORD and determines to go despite the fears and objections of his men (1 Samuel 23:1-5).

David, the giant slayer, inspired great warriors. His patriotic and Godly vision gave purpose to the battle. 1 Chronicles 11:10-12:40 lists the warriors who surrounded David in the wilderness and helped to establish him when he became king. It should be obvious that many of these men would never have become great without the inspiration of David leading them. The list starts with Jashobeam who killed three hundred men in a single battle. Abishai did the same (1 Chronicles 11:20). Benaiah killed a giant (1 Chronicles 11:23). As David's kingdom is established his warriors will kill several more giants. There is nothing like a giant slayer to inspire giant slayers.

David listened to advice and kept the best advisors around him, but when the advice he got didn't seem right, or the issue was too important to decide lightly, he always sought the Chief Advisor. Time and time again we see David calling for the Ephod or getting apart to 'refresh himself in the LORD'. He knew that some things only God could answer. David trusted that he would get the right answer if he sought God's will. Even in the matter of whether or not to leave the territory of the Philistine's and to return to Judah after the death of Saul, David asked God, "shall I go?", and if so "to which [city]?" (2 Samuel 2:1). Given the circumstances, would we have even thought to ask?

Live Well in the Wilderness

David's attitude, his anointing, his willingness to listen to advise, even harsh advice, and David's quickness to inquire into God's advice all stem from one thing: David's relationship with God. This is seen in the psalm's, many of which we have seen were written in David's dark days in the wilderness. In complaint, in fear, in anger and upset, David always stayed close to God. He always believed that God was his friend.

From the beginning of David's trial in the wilderness we see his heart displayed in the Psalms. David flees unprepared and without clear plans. His first stop, as we saw, was a visit to the priests of Nob who helped him on his way. Unfortunately, Doeg the Edomite sees David there and runs to tell Saul who kills all but one of the priests. In Psalm 52, David has harsh words for Doeg actions, but finishes the psalm by refocusing on his relationship with God: "But as for me, I am like a green olive tree in the house of God; I trust in the lovingkindness of God forever and ever. I will give You thanks forever, because You have done it, And I will wait on Your name, for it is good, in the presence of Your godly ones" (Psalm 52:8-9).

Soon, David finds himself in trouble in Gath where the Philistines have recognized him. He manages to escape, but his problems haven't gone away. He admits to feeling watched and hunted (Psalm 56:1-2, 5-6) and to fear (Psalm 56:3). I can almost see him in prayer, behind a bush, rocking and praying in the peculiar way Jews do: "In God, whose word I praise, In the LORD, whose word I praise, In God I have put my trust, I shall not be afraid. What can man do to me? Your vows are binding upon me, O God; I will render thank offerings to You. For You have delivered my soul from death, Indeed my feet from stumbling, So that I may walk before God In the light of the living" (Psalm 56:10-13).

The notes proceeding the psalms tell us that both Psalm 56 and Psalm 34 were written in response to David's brush with death there in Gath. Psalm 56 has the urgency of someone whose heart is still beating fast. Psalm 34 reads like he has had time to calm down and reflect. In it, David soars lyric in his celebration of what God has done. There are great lines that have leant themselves to song: "Oh, taste and see that the LORD is good!" (Psalm 34:8), and "Those who look to him are radiant, and their faces are never ashamed" (Psalm 34:5). In other words, the more David thinks about it, the happier he gets, until he just has to sing. David has not suddenly wandered onto easy street. He is simply seeing that God is there with him, protecting him.

His trials in the wilderness will continue for another 12 or 13 years. During this time, he writes several more psalms some of which are notated as having been written during this period. Psalm 54 is short thank you for rescue: "I will give thanks to Your name, O LORD, for it is good" (Psalm 54:6). Psalm 57 shows how he is making spiritual warfare: "My heart is steadfast, O God, my heart is steadfast; I will sing, yes, I will sing praises! Awake, my glory! Awake, harp and lyre! I will awaken the dawn. I will give thanks to You, O Lord, among the peoples; I will sing praises to You among the nations" (Psalm 57:7-9). And what can be said about Psalm 63. Three thousand years later, it makes a great contemporary worship song: "O God, You are my God; I shall seek You earnestly; My soul thirsts for You, my flesh yearns for You, In a dry and weary land where there is no water" (Psalm 63:1). And finally Psalm 142 is a woeful prayer at a particularly difficult time:

"Give heed to my cry, For I am brought very low" (Psalm 142:6). Dozens more of the psalms of David read as if they were also written during his time in the wilderness, or on remembering those times.

Remembering

There are two psalms of special interest at the moment when David's time of trial in the wilderness has ended. One the Song of the Bow, which David instructed be taught to all of Judah (2 Samuel 1:18), and Psalm 18, a psalm written after Saul has died and David returns to Israel.

Let's look at Psalm 18 first. It has none of the wild and honest emotionalism of the psalms written in the wilderness. It could well have been written as an inaugural statement upon taking the throne of Judah: "You have delivered me from the contentions of the people; You have placed me as head of the nations; A people whom I have not known serve me" (Psalm 18:43); and "He gives great deliverance to His king, And shows lovingkindness to His anointed, To David and his descendants forever" (Psalm 18:50). The poetry is grand: "The LORD is my rock and my fortress and my deliverer" (Psalm 18:2). "Then the earth shook and quaked; And the foundations of the mountains were trembling And were shaken, because He was angry" (Psalm 18:7). "For by You I can run upon a troop; And by my God I can leap over a wall" (Psalm 18:29). "He makes my feet like hinds' feet, And sets me upon my high places" (Psalm 18:33). The entire psalm paints a picture of David's close relationship with God, David's travails, God's fierce defense all in brilliant brush strokes. There is no mention of David's fears, his despondency or his anger. The psalm is a fine tribute to the king taking the throne, but we miss the personal touch that makes so many of the psalms so special.

The 'Song of the Bow', found in 2 Samuel Chapter 1, is different. It must have been written at about the same time, but the tone is entirely different. Saul had spent well over a decade pursuing David to kill him, but David is unable to hate Saul but rather laments his death: "Your beauty, O Israel, is slain on your high places! How have the mighty fallen!" (2 Samuel 1:19). He pronounces a curse over mountains of Gilboa: "O mountains of Gilboa, Let not dew or rain be on you, nor fields of offerings" (2 Samuel 1:21). According to Derek Prince, the Israeli government has had a successful tree planting program through Israel, except on Mount Gilboa. For some unexplainable reason the trees won't prosper there. "Saul and Jonathan, beloved and pleasant in their life, And in their death they were not parted; They were swifter than eagles, They were stronger than lions" (2 Samuel 1:23). David, unlike Saul, has no fear or jealousy about extolling the greatness of those around him, or those who proceeded him. He perfectly shared honor where honor was due.

Discussion Points:

1. How do we see David embracing his anointing, even when kingship seemed far away?

2. Thinking of the advice around David in the wilderness, how does he keep on the right track?

3. How does David's attitude inspire greatness?

4. Saul failed in many ways. Why does David honor him as God's anointed?

Application:

1. David was placed on a very clear path of providence. For many years, however, that path seemed like an impossible dream. And yet, David continued to act in a way appropriate to his destiny, until the day his destiny began to fall into place. Do you feel that you have a destiny? Is it near or far? What do you do when it is still far off?

2. We know that David had a lot of bad advice given to him throughout his life. In many cases, he had few or no reliable sources of advice. We see that time and time again, he separated himself to get with God so he could get the right answer for the moment. How do you filter the advice you get now? Would you like to change that?

3. David was able to inspire men to do things that they didn't want to do. He was able to lead men successfully when they were angry with him and wanted to stone him. Do your attitudes inspire greatness? Is there something you can do to improve that?

4. Saul had been discarded by God, but David was still able to honor his memory for what he did do well. When someone close to you fails in many ways, are you able to see the good in them still? Are you able to speak well of the good they have done, or are doing?